Spotlight on the MAYA, AZTEC, and INCA CIVILIZATIONS

The Ancient AZTEC ECONOMY

Barbara M. Linde

PowerKiDS press

NEW YORK

Published in 2017 by The Rosen Publishing Group, Inc.
29 East 21st Street, New York, NY 10010

Editor: Katie Kawa
Book Design: Tanya Dellaccio

Photo Credits: Cover, pp. 8-9 https://commons.wikimedia.org/wiki/File:La_Gran_Tenochtitlan.JPG; p. 4 https://commons.wikimedia.org/wiki/File:Reconstruction_of_Tenochtitlan2006.jpg; p. 5 https://commons.wikimedia.org/wiki/File:Mexico_City_Zocalo_Cathedral.jpg; p. 7 (top) https://commons.wikimedia.org/wiki/File:Codex_Mendoza_folio_62r.jpg; p. 7 (bottom) https://commons.wikimedia.org/wiki/File:Codex_Mendoza_folio_60r.jpg; p. 9 https://commons.wikimedia.org/wiki/File:Codex_Mendoza_folio_47r.jpg; p. 11 De Agostini Picture Library/Getty Images; p. 13 https://commons.wikimedia.org/wiki/File:Tlatelolco_Marketplace.JPG; p. 14 Valentyn Volkov/Shutterstock.com; p. 15 Universal History Archive/Getty Images; p. 17 Werner Forman/Getty Images; p. 18 (both) https://commons.wikimedia.org/wiki/File:The_Florentine_Codex-_Agriculture.tiff; p. 19 Heritage Images/Getty Images; p. 21 https://commons.wikimedia.org/wiki/File:Codex_Mendoza_folio_37r.jpg; p. 22 OMAR TORRES/Getty Images; p. 23 https://commons.wikimedia.org/wiki/File:Aztecs_storing_maize.jpg; pp. 24–25 De Agostini / G. Dagli Orti/Getty Images; p. 26 Dorling Kindersley/Getty Images; p. 27 (both) Dario Lo Presti/Shutterstock.com; p. 28 https://commons.wikimedia.org/wiki/File:Feather_headdress_Moctezuma_II.JPG; p. 29 https://commons.wikimedia.org/wiki/File:Nezahualpiltzintli.jpg.

Library of Congress Cataloging-in-Publication Data

Names: Linde, Barbara M., author.
Title: The ancient Aztec economy / Barbara M. Linde.
Description: New York : PowerKids Press, 2016. | Series: Spotlight on the Maya, Aztec, and Inca civilizations | Includes index.
Identifiers: LCCN 2016002136 | ISBN 9781499419054 (pbk.) | ISBN 9781499419078 (library bound) | ISBN 9781508148982 (6 pack)
Subjects: LCSH: Aztecs--Economic conditions. | Aztecs--Commerce. | Indians of Mexico--Economic conditions. | Indians of Mexico--Commerce--History--To 1500.
Classification: LCC F1219.76.E36 L56 2016 | DDC 972/.01--dc23
LC record available at http://lccn.loc.gov/2016002136

CPSIA Compliance Information: Batch #BS16PK: For further information contact Rosen Publishing, New York, New York at 1-800-237-9932.

CONTENTS

THE AZTEC EMPIRE

The Aztec people created an advanced civilization and powerful empire in what's now central and southern Mexico. The Aztec Empire flourished during the 14th, 15th, and 16th centuries. Historians believe the Aztecs called themselves the Mexica. The name "Aztec" wasn't used until much later.

The early Aztec people settled on an island in Lake Texcoco. They built their main city, Tenochtitlán, on the

MODEL OF TENOCHTITLÁN

The Aztec Empire was made up of **city-states**, with Tenochtitlán being the most powerful. Today, the Mexican capital of Mexico City is located where Tenochtitlán once stood.

marshy land found there. This city grew to become the center of the Aztec Empire. The Aztec people were fierce warriors who conquered other groups of people around them. Over time, the Aztec Empire grew rich and powerful.

Three things helped the Aztec Empire expand and stay strong. Trade helped people get all the goods they needed. Everyone paid taxes or **tributes** to the empire. Agriculture, or farming, was important for feeding the people. These three factors allowed the Aztec people to develop a prosperous economy.

THE MARKET SYSTEM

The Aztec Empire was a trade-based economy. Producers made goods. Merchants bought the goods and then sold them to consumers. Every town and village had at least one marketplace, or *tianquiztli*. The main market was in a central spot close to the temple. In some city-states, the markets were open every day. Otherwise, the markets were open on a set **schedule** of days.

The marketplace was at the center of Aztec social life and economic activity. People traded goods at this bustling, busy place. They met with old friends and made new friends. They heard the latest news about their neighbors, the city-state, and the empire.

People came to the markets by boat or on foot. Some Aztec people traveled many miles to visit the closest marketplace. The Aztec people didn't have wagons or horses, so **porters** carried all the merchants' goods with special frames or in large baskets. Consumers carried their purchases the same way.

Shown here is part of a codex, or book of ancient writing, depicting Aztec people carrying goods on their back and in a canoe.

GOODS IN THE MARKETPLACE

Markets carried everything the Aztec people needed or wanted: food, clothing, jewelry, medicine, and more. A buyer could get food supplies—including meats, tortillas, fish, and seeds—in one section. Then, they could move to another section for clothing. Builders might be in another area, buying bricks and wood. Crafters showed off their skills and sold their wares. Ceramic goods were popular items to buy and sell in Aztec marketplaces. The Aztec people also produced textiles, or fabrics, to sell.

This painting shows a crowded area of Tenochtitlán with many people coming together to trade and talk.

Over time, some markets became famous for just one or a few things. People from all over the empire would go to these markets to get special items. For example, Coyoacán's market specialized in products made of wood. Acolman was known as the place to buy dogs that Aztec people used as food. Azcapotzalco was the site of a famous Aztec slave market.

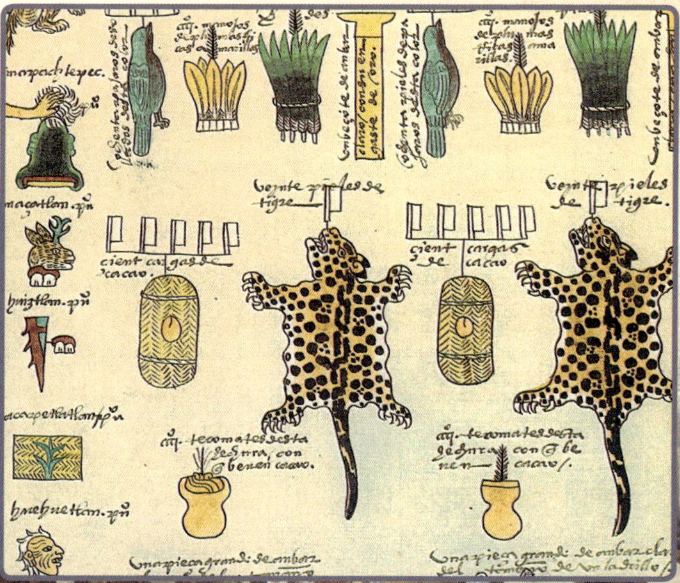

Some of the goods found throughout the Aztec Empire can be seen in the codex page shown here.

MARKETPLACE RULES

The leader of the city-state was in charge of the market. His superintendent, or manager, collected fees from the merchants. Inspectors were always on duty. They carefully checked the quality of the goods being sold in the market. If a merchant tried to sell items that were poorly made or food that wasn't fresh, he was punished. The same fate awaited merchants who tried to cheat buyers using incorrect measurements. Officials also walked through Aztec markets to keep the peace and prevent **disturbances**, such as theft.

Judges in a special marketplace court tried cases related to what happened in the markets. If someone was convicted of theft and found guilty, they faced harsh punishments. The thief might be fined or even put to death. The court also listened to merchants who had disagreements. Then, the judges would decide how to handle the problem.

Shown here is part of a codex depicting Aztec leadership. The top image shows a leader talking to those who worked under him. The bottom image shows Aztec judges.

THE TLATELOLCO MARKETPLACE

The city of Tlatelolco was next to Tenochtitlán. It's sometimes called Tenochtitlán's sister city. The main marketplace in Tlatelolco was the largest marketplace in the Aztec Empire. On some days, as many as 60,000 people crowded onto its busy streets. When the Spanish arrived in Aztec lands, they were amazed by the Tlatelolco marketplace. They described it in great detail in their writings.

Both Tenochtitlán and Tlatelolco were island cities. The water around them was crowded with canoes coming to and going from the market. Other visitors walked across the **causeways** from the mainland. Some merchants sold goods made within the Aztec Empire. Others sold goods from distant regions. People were able to buy the things they needed, such as cooking pots and simple foods. Wealthier Aztecs could buy luxuries, or things they wanted but didn't need. Fancy feathers, decorated clothing, and jewelry were all for sale.

Shown here is a model from the Field Museum of Natural History in Chicago, Illinois. It was created to show what the Tlatelolco marketplace is believed to have looked like at the height of the Aztec Empire.

CHOCOLATE AND COTTON CURRENCY

The ancient Aztec people didn't have coins or paper **currency** like we use today. Instead, the Aztec people often used cacao beans or seeds to buy things. Today, we use cacao beans for a different purpose—to make cocoa and chocolate! The Aztecs also used these beans to make a kind of chocolate drink, but they were especially valuable as currency.

Other ancient civilizations in North America and Central America, including the Maya, also used cacao beans, shown here, as a form of currency.

TAJADERO

Quachtli was a form of Aztec currency made from cotton. The cotton was woven into cloth. Then, it was cut into large pieces. Some historical sources state that a family that had about 20 lengths of *quachtli* could live comfortably for a whole year in Tenochtitlán. Both the size and quality of *quachtli* determined its value. The same was true of cacao beans.

A *tajadero* was a piece of metal that looked like a hoe. The Aztecs used this as a form of currency, too.

MERCHANTS

The Aztec marketplaces couldn't exist without merchants. There were two groups of merchants in Aztec society. The local merchants stayed close to home. Some sold food their family members grew. Local merchants sold pottery and other family-made crafts, too.

The *pochteca* were a special group of traveling merchants. They transported goods all over the Aztec Empire. They also went to regions beyond the borders of the Aztec Empire. These merchants took Aztec goods to sell to other groups. They brought back rare and unusual items that couldn't be found in the Aztec Empire. Sometimes the *pochteca* were gone for months or even years.

Wars sometimes broke out if a traveling Aztec merchant was harmed or threatened. These merchants were viewed as a valuable part of the empire. While they were trading, the *pochteca* sometimes spied on neighboring groups. Were the people rich? Were they weak? The *pochteca* told Aztec leaders everything they found out.

Shown here is a page of a codex describing Aztec merchants. At the top left is the Aztec god of merchants. At the top right is a picture of an Aztec merchant on a journey.

SOCIAL CLASSES

Ancient Aztec society was divided into two main social classes. Economic factors played a big part in the division of these social classes.

One class in Aztec society was the nobility. Religious, political, and military leaders were part of the nobility, along with lords, or landowners. The leader of each city-state was the highest noble under the emperor, who was the leader of the whole empire. The emperor gave land to other nobles. They passed it on through their families. The nobles had many luxuries.

These images from a codex show Aztec commoners working the land.

Most Aztec people were commoners, including the merchants. They lived in small homes on a noble's land. Common people paid nobles in crops, goods, and services. Male commoners served as warriors. No one earned wages for their work. Instead, they were able to keep some of the crops they grew or things they made. Commoners could become slaves as a punishment or a way to pay a debt or tax. They could sometimes buy their own freedom.

Shown here is Montezuma II, who was an Aztec emperor. His high standing in Aztec society is shown in his decorative clothing and feathered headdress. These were luxuries only wealthy nobles could afford.

TAXES AND TRIBUTES

Commoners paid taxes that supported the nobles, including the leader of their city-state. Nobles didn't have to pay taxes.

Commoners used *quachtli* to pay taxes to their lords. Other goods and services could also be provided as payment. Farmers gave part of their food to the landowners. Women wove clothing for nobles. **Artisans** and merchants in the marketplaces paid taxes, too. The amount and the type of payment was recorded, and some of these records still exist today.

A conquered tribe paid a large tribute to the Aztec emperor. This might have been food, gold, weapons, or other goods. Once a city-state was part of the Aztec Empire, it had to send tributes a certain number of times each year. Collectors, whom the Aztec people called *calpixque*, made sure people made their payments to the empire. Failure to pay could lead to punishments, including being sentenced to slavery.

This page from a codex shows a list of tributes paid to the Aztec emperor. There are clothes, grain, gold, wood, and other items.

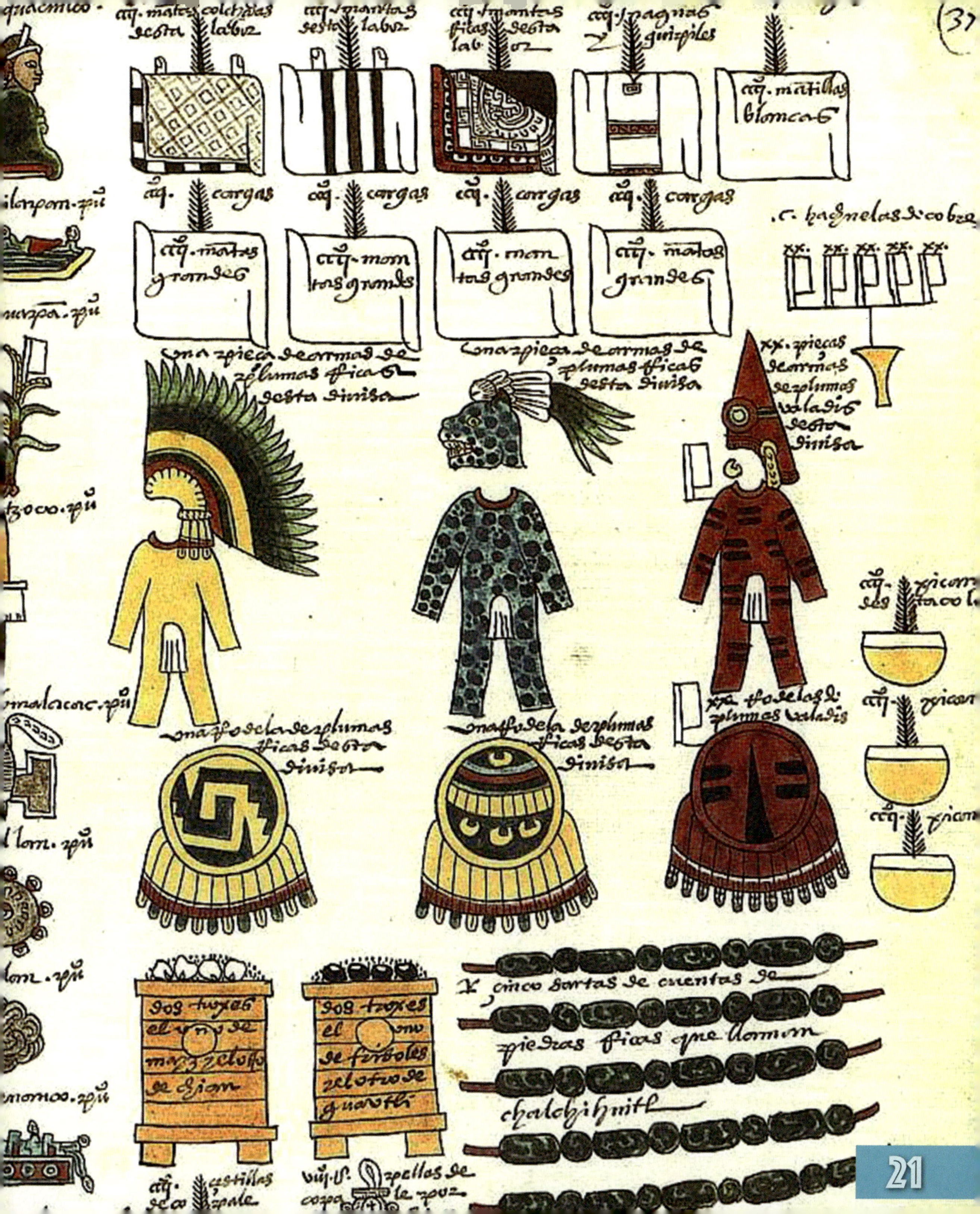
una pieça de armas de plumas ricas desta divisa
una pieça de armas de plumas ricas desta divisa
xx. pieças de armas de plumas valadis desta divisa
una rodela de plumas ricas desta divisa
una rodela de plumas ricas desta divisa
cinco sartas de cuentas de piedras ricas que llaman chalchihuitl

THE IMPORTANCE OF FARMING

Farming was the most important occupation in the Aztec Empire because its citizens needed to be fed. The Aztec Empire was able to become powerful and successful because of its strong agricultural foundation. Farming was the base from which the Aztec economy grew. The empire couldn't exist without crops from its many farms.

Chinampas, such as the ones shown here, were one of the many ways Aztec farmers used their surroundings to improve the economy. Chinampas are gardens made to float on a lake.

The nobles owned the land, but the common farmers worked it. The job of tending this land was often passed down through the farmer's family. Children began helping in the fields at an early age.

Maize, or corn, was the most important crop for the Aztecs. Beans, squash, avocados, tomatoes, and chili peppers were also grown. Some farmers raised animals for food. On market days, members of the farmer's family took their extra crops to the marketplace.

Crop failure could lead to a food shortage in the empire, and it could limit trade. Farmers developed many creative ways to get water and improve the soil.

Maize could be stored to use at a later date. That's what this image from the Florentine Codex shows.

JOBS FOR EVERYONE

A strong labor force was essential to the development of the Aztec economy. Everyone worked—even young children. Farmers grew crops. Talented artisans made baskets and pottery. There were Aztecs who made tools and musical instruments. Sculptors created statues of real people and Aztec gods. Teaching was an important job because all Aztec children went to school.

The nobles ran the government and served as judges. Nobles also managed their lands. The ruler of a city-state maintained order. He also made sure the taxes were collected.

Aztec priests had plenty of work to do. The highest priests were nobles, but commoners could also be priests. They worked in the temples and prepared religious ceremonies. Some priests taught the children of nobles.

Aztec women also had their own jobs to do. Women and girls wove cloth for clothing. Women could also work in the marketplace or serve as priestesses.

Because religion was such an important part of Aztec life, priests and priestesses had respected jobs in the empire.

THE MILITARY

A strong military was an important part of the Aztec economy. Aztec warriors protected the empire from invasion. War helped the empire grow. When the fierce Aztec warriors defeated an enemy, their land became part of the Aztec Empire. The conquered people then began paying tribute to the Aztec emperor.

AZTEC WARRIORS

War was one way the Aztec Empire grew larger and richer. This made warriors valuable to both the Aztec government and the Aztec economy.

The empire didn't need a large army all the time. Only military leaders had permanent jobs. They trained boys to become warriors. The boys trained until they were adults. When there was a need, these men left their other work and formed a powerful army.

Aztec warriors weren't paid. However, they received other rewards if they were successful, such as clothing, land, or slaves. Serving as a warrior was a way for an Aztec man to move up in society. Even a common man could become a member of the noble class if he was a successful warrior.

FOOD, DRINK, AND DRESS

It was easy to tell the classes apart by looking at members of Aztec society. Nobles and commoners wore different clothes to reflect their social and economic **status**. Only nobles were allowed to wear cotton. They could also decorate their clothing with feathers, beads, or jewels. **Turquoise** was a luxury only available to the highest members of Aztec society, such as the emperor.

This feathered headdress is believed to have been worn by the Aztec emperor Montezuma II.

Shown here is an image of an Aztec ruler. It's easy to tell he was part of the noble class because of his bold and colorful clothing.

Instead of cotton, commoners used cloth made from the maguey plant for their clothing. This cloth was of a lower quality than cotton cloth, and it wasn't as comfortable to wear. Commoners couldn't wear fancy clothes or bright colors.

Different foods and drinks were available to different groups of Aztec people based on their social class. For example, commoners mainly drank water. However, nobles could enjoy a drink made from cacao beans.

UNCOVERING THE AZTEC EMPIRE

The Aztec Empire fell to the Spanish **conquistadors** around 1521 with the conquest of Tenochtitlán. The Spanish kept written records during this time. They wrote a lot about the Aztec people and their way of life. They drew pictures of the people and their cities. The Aztec people also wrote about their empire. The Spanish kept some of these writings. Certain archaeologists and historians can read the old Aztec writing. It has revealed much about the Aztec people, including their economy.

Over time, the Spanish settlers built over most of the old Aztec city-states. Now, archaeologists are digging up the ruins. They study the tools, broken bits of pottery, and other things they find. These artifacts are helping historians learn about Aztec farming, Aztec trade, and many other aspects of their economy and society.

We're learning more about the ancient Aztecs with every new artifact found, but there is still much more to discover!

GLOSSARY

artisan (AAR-tuh-zuhn): A skilled worker who makes things with their hands.

causeway (KOZ-way): A raised road across wet ground or water.

city-state (SIH-tee–STAYT): A self-governing state made up of a city and surrounding lands.

conquistador (kahn-KEES-tuh-dor): A Spanish person who conquered, or took over, people and land, especially in the Americas during the 16th century.

currency (KUHR-uhn-see): Money.

disturbance (dihs-TUHR-buhns): A breakdown of peaceful and law-abiding behavior.

porter (POR-tuhr): A person who carries things for another person.

schedule (SKEH-jool): A list of times when certain events will happen.

status (STAA-tuhs): Position or rank in relation to others.

tribute (TRIH-byoot): Payment by one ruler or nation to another as the price of peace.

turquoise (TUHR-koyz): A blue or bluish-green mineral used in jewelry.

INDEX

PRIMARY SOURCE LIST

Page 7 (top): Folio 62 of the Codex Mendoza. Creator unknown. ca. 1542. Now kept at the Bodleian Library, Oxford University, Oxford, UK.

Page 7 (bottom): Folio 60 of the Codex Mendoza. Creator unknown. ca. 1542. Now kept at the Bodleian Library, Oxford University, Oxford, UK.

Page 11: Page from the Florentine Codex. Compiled by Fray Bernardino de Sahagún. ca. 1529–1588. Now kept at the Laurentian Library, Florence, Italy.

Page 18 (both): Page from the Florentine Codex. Compiled by Fray Bernardino de Sahagún. ca. 1529–1588. Now kept at the Laurentian Library, Florence, Italy.

WEBSITES

Due to the changing nature of Internet links, PowerKids Press has developed an online list of websites related to the subject of this book. This site is updated regularly. Please use this link to access the list: www.powerkidslinks.com/soac/azecon